To Barb,
From

MW00937123

Jesus vs. Santa

Christmas Misunderstood

The Misunderstood Series

May the Gift
of Christmas Remain
Alive in Your Life!

Jason E. Royle

Copyright © 2015 Jason E. Royle

All rights reserved worldwide

No part of this publication may be made publicly available,
reproduced, or copied/sold in any form whatsoever without the
express written consent of the author.

Illustrations by: Cormac Mac Ateer
Formatting by: Polgarus Studio

Requests for permission should be addressed to:
J. E. Royle, Box 283, Schaefferstown, PA 17088
or emailed to roylejason@gmail.com.

Connect with Jason
On Twitter @ JERoyle
Blog @ www.jasonroyle.net

CONTENTS

Chapter 1
The Battle for Christmas

If you had to pick a side, whose would it be, Jesus' or Santa's? Be honest. Every year we force the two undisputed champions of winter to duke it out to see which one is the more generous, more perfect symbol of Christmas. Of course we award the Christ child with the title every year, but I suspect he wins because we feel a sense of loyalty to our traditions, and not because we really believe he is the best representation of his own birthday celebration. After all, birthdays are about fun with friends and gifts—lots of gifts. The only people at Jesus' birthday party were some sheep-herding strangers and an assortment of barn-yard animals. Maybe that's why one of the three gifts he received was incense?

Let's face it. When it comes to divvying out worldly possessions, Santa's marketing department is doing a great job. He has more to give, much more, or so it seems. I submit to you that if we really believed Jesus alone was enough, Santa would have faded into the background a long time ago, and there would be no battle for the Christmas limelight. But that didn't happen.

Every year, around the same time of year, with the start of the Christmas season, many people go back to worrying about the battle, or as some like to call it, the "War on Christmas." The battle, for some, is that Christ—the reason for the season—is being removed from Christmas and the moral and spiritual consciousness of society is in steep decline because of it.

The war on Christmas is real. It has to be won. But with all due respect, can anyone tell me what it's really all about? Or how it even started? Instead of enjoying Jesus and Santa, we inevitably pick a side: the churchgoers versus the non-churchgoers, the Christians versus the media. Is Santa just innocent fun? Or is he, after taking the "n" and sliding it to the end, really just *Satan* in disguise?

Is it okay to celebrate both? If Christmas falls on a Sunday, are we exempt from having to go to church since it's a holiday? While it may be a season teeming with joy and toys, it also marks the beginning of the battle: when our children are bombarded with the secular versus the sacred aspects of Christmas.

As Christian parents, where do we draw the line when it comes to what we consider to be real versus what we consider to be make-believe? The debate seems clear and straightforward, but upon closer examination, it quickly gets messy and turns mysterious. It is our Christian duty to guard the sacred gate of our children's innocent minds and give no room for the wicked ways of the world to distort them, is it not? So let the battle begin:

"In one corner we have Kris Kringle, known to many as Saint Nicholas. Once a fourth-century Catholic bishop, now he

is more commonly known as the slightly overweight, white-bearded, jolly old man dressed in a red suit who likes to give gifts to children. It's Saaaaanta Claus.

"In the other corner, we have Emmanuel, known to many as God's Son. Once a carpenter, he is remembered most affectionately for his teachings and his miracles: walking on water, feeding five thousand, healing the sick, and, of course, history's greatest party trick ever—turning water into wine. It's Jeee-sus Chriiiiiiiist!"

When we put it like that, it seems a little ridiculous to stick them in a ring like two combat warriors, but we do it every year. Without reservation, I will be the first pastor to admit—I'm not one hundred percent opposed to Santa Claus—but I'm not totally in favor of him either. I can see why so many Christians are uncomfortable with the Santa tradition. No parent wants to make Santa out to be another God in the minds of their children. But in the grand scheme of things, does Santa Claus really ruin the Christian celebration of the birth of Jesus Christ, totally? I'm not convinced he does.

> Is it possible to view the traditions of Christmas in a way that complements, rather than hinders our celebration?

I get it: The Santa legend is a cruel fabrication—a far-fetched, delusional lie perpetuated by parents who preach to their children not to lie! To the child, there's no problem that a little imagination can't solve. Just how will Santa get into the house if there is no chimney? How will he keep from becoming overheated in Texas weather? How will his sleigh function without snow? After drinking all that milk and eating all those cookies, does Santa ever take a restroom break? These questions pose little concern to young minds.

It takes almost no effort to make a child believe in Santa Claus. Step one: put some presents under a Christmas tree every year. Step two: tell the child that Santa put them there. Result: you've got a Santa-believer on your hands, and you have tradition to thank for it.

To the adult, Santa is a weird, white-glove-wearing magic man. If the Odin thing holds up (we'll talk more about this later), that would actually make him Thor's dad. At worst, he's the ghost of Saint Nicholas. At best, he's an elf-like fairy. It can all be very confusing. And, at times, even feel like we're tiptoeing around the fringe of being downright paganistic. I think we're all wondering the same thing here:

Is Santa a family-friendly avatar, or is he a dangerous gateway that leads children into something potentially diabolical?

If we want to raise our children to be grounded, productive citizens of God's green earth, I think we all eventually get to the point where we decide it's time for Santa to die (in our children's eyes, that is). Yes. Think about it. Sooner or later, we all end up killing off Santa.

But *how* we kill him off is the issue. Are we killing Santa because he's not real or because he's anti-Christian? Is there a universe where Savior and Santa can peacefully coexist? After all, we use Santa-like qualities to help us reinforce Jesus-like behavior in our children all the time. Look at all they have in common—

Santa, like God, is all-knowing—he knows what kind of toy every little girl and boy in the world wants. Santa, like God, is a moral judge—rewarding the good with a gift, and rewarding the bad with a lump of coal. Santa, like God, is omnipresent—he can be everywhere in the world during the same night of the year.

Both Jesus and Santa have workers dedicated to their cause. Both are heroes of their own stories, unfathomable characters outside the realm of logic. Both have characteristics that are admired and understood. Both have many other qualities that are mysterious and equally *misunderstood*. It sounds to me like Jesus and Santa would have a lot to talk about.

So, let's talk about it.

Chapter 2
Dear Santa

"Dear Santa…" the soft voice of my three-year-old drifted in from the living room. So I got up to look in on her. And, to my surprise, what did I see? Her kneeling at the Christmas tree with her hands folded. She was in her official three-year-old prayer pose. "…please bring me a new puppy, a yellow ball, a green bicycle, and…" Oh my goodness! She's *praying*…to…SANTA!

I rushed over to her side. "No. No. No. We do not pray to Santa! We pray to Jesus." I was clear. I was direct. She knew I was serious. A week later, up went the nativity and my daughter had questions.

"What are those three men doing?" she asked of the ceramic nativity display.

"They're bringing gifts to baby Jesus," my wife explained.

"Oh, so Jesus can take the gifts to Santa and Santa can bring them to us," our daughter said, trying her best to connect the dots. A few days later, we were all together on a family drive and she finally blurted out the profound truth, however confusing it seemed to her. "So, Dad." "Yes?" I replied. "We can see Santa and the Easter Bunny," she said, "but we can't see God or Jesus." My jaw dropped.

I paused before speaking. *What's going on here? How did*

she figure that out? Why is she even thinking like this? My precious little girl, what have I done to you? She had been working so hard to string together this scattering of visible (and invisible) dots in an effort to save her parents (in her mind) from being nothing but a couple of liars! Agh! She was on to us. Busted with nowhere to hide.

I am a preacher of the gospel, not a minister of, "you better be good for goodness' sake." My daughter wasn't looking for an answer. As far as she knew, she didn't even have a question. She was making a declaration. And good thing too, because I couldn't come up with a quick answer that would clearly clarify the traditions my wife and I had been teaching her with regard to the relationship that exists between Christianity, the church, Jesus Christ, and Santa Claus.

My wife and I had been doing things according to the way we've always done them. How we were raised. Little did we know that the only thing we were doing was perpetuating a cycle. We read books. We prayed. We asked our parents what to do. We were doing everything we knew to do to prevent the faith of our little girl from being tainted by the ways of the world.

Surely to goodness other parents and families out there know what I'm talking about. Once I realized my daughter could not distinguish between Santa and Jesus and the roles each played in the holiday festivities, I had to ask myself some serious questions about religion, fantasy, and our beloved traditions.

How do we teach our children the differences
between the sacred realities of Jesus
and the secular traditions of Santa?

In that one moment, when my three year-old daughter stopped just short of challenging whether or not Jesus is real, I discovered something rather troubling. Like it or not, 52 weeks of church attendance can quickly be undone in just 32 days. Through what is called the Christmas season (which seems to grow longer every year), Santa is blasted into the minds of our children. Computer games portray him, movies are made about him, songs remind us of him, and shopping malls give us an opportunity to meet him. Seriously, are my wife and I dropping the ball as parents here, or are we all just victims of slick ad campaigns that are here today and gone tomorrow?

My parents never explained to me the differences between Jesus and Santa. I don't remember there being any real need for them to do so. My dad never had to sit me down for "the talk" (not that kind of talk, but a Christmas talk).

I can hear him now: "Son, Santa is not real. Yes, I know you can go sit on his lap and have your picture made with him at the mall, but he doesn't exist. You know who is real? Invisible Jesus. That's who we serve. That's who we love. That's why you're in that Christmas play at church. Now go tell your sister to hurry up and get in here. Supper is on the table and it's her turn to pray."

Never happened.

So why is it that, one generation later, I am faced with a problem my father never faced? I think the culprit is overexposure. Round-the-clock programming both on and off the tube has led to a Christmastime cancer that is now my generation's responsibility to correct. Who should I blame for this twisted theology sweeping across our land, contaminating innocent minds? To whom should I address my strongly worded letter: my parents, the media, the Church?

In his famous study in human nature, William James provides remarkable insight into "The Reality of the Unseen." He says: "All our attitudes—moral, practical, or emotional, as well as religious—are due to the objects of our consciousness, the things which we believe to exist, whether really or ideally." James goes on to say, "Such objects may be present to our senses, or they may be present only to our thought. In either case they elicit from us a reaction; and the reaction due to things of thought is notoriously in many cases as strong as that due to sensible presences. It may even be stronger" (The Varieties of Religious Experience, Lecture III, Edinburgh, 1901–1902).

In other words, our minds create our realities. We treat ideas that are real in our minds with the same gravity we treat tangible objects. So, if our kids are bombarded with traditional Christmas marketing, they are going to think about Santa and his sleigh full of goodies. Jesus, on the other hand, is typically out of sight and out of mind during the Christmas season. Ironic, isn't it?

Santa dominates the hearts and minds of children in much the same way Jesus dominates the hearts and minds of his followers. It's true. If, however, we can *reposition* Jesus in the minds of our children and look for ways to neutralize the effects of the barrage of Christmas ads between November and December, Jesus and Santa stand a chance at having a peaceful coexistence.

We can't just stand by and let nature take its course.

We have to do something.

But what?

As a pastor, I am an eye witness to the shifting dynamics of the Church. I see families fragmenting, technology expanding, and materialism growing. I guess what I didn't expect to see was faith wavering, hope hesitating, and love growing cold. Every day there seem to be more questions than answers, more moral concerns than spiritual solutions.

So what do we do?

> **Remember:** Religion and tradition are both very personal experiences. We adopt them as we see fit, and this differs from person to person, family to family, church to church. Through much thought and prayer, it is up to each of us to decide what works best for us and our family in accordance with our interpretation of God's will and purpose for our lives.

Recognize: What is problematic and worrisome for you may not be a big deal for your child.

Remember: How we react often speaks as clearly as words, and sometimes even more clearly.

Recognize: Your love, not your worry, is the most valuable thing any of us can give our children.

Chapter 3
The December Duo: Illustrated

We humans like to fix things. We spend massive amounts of time and energy in "fix-it mode," repairing things that we think need to be fixed. With so many of us having adopted "fix it" as our default setting, it's no wonder we sometimes forget that life can be fun. Now, here's a thought: What if Jesus versus Santa is not something that can be fixed? What then? The history is what it is. Santa is who he is. We're not in the business of fixing Santa Claus. Retailers are not in the business of being Christian evangelists. Retailers simply want your business, no matter who you are.

Our mission is to gain insight so that we can understand and make a decision on how to keep Santa in his own lane so our kids don't end up sending letters to Jesus at the North Pole and praying to Santa under the Christmas tree.

For once, let's not focus all our attention on fixing it. For the next few minutes, let's just let Santa be Santa and Jesus be Jesus. Let's pull back the reins of opinion, take a step back from all defensive measures, and let's just have some fun.

What soap is to the body, laughter is to the soul.
—*Yiddish proverb*

You think Jesus and Santa have nothing in common? Think again! Over the next several pages, we are going to take a playful look at a handful of out-of-the-ordinary comparisons between the once-a-year gift-giver, and the giver of the ultimate eternal gift.

With a twinkle of the eye and a smile on your face, I hope you enjoy these amusing comparisons of the December Duo.

***

Jesus is a carpenter.

—Mark 6:3

Santa is a carpenter...of toys.

Jesus will return like a thief in the night.

—Luke12:39–40

Santa enters homes like a thief in the night.

Jesus is the sovereign Lord of hosts.

—Psalm 24:10

Santa is sovereign lord over a host of elves.

Jesus expects us to
ask God in heaven for good gifts.
—*Matthew 7:11*

Santa expects us to
just be happy with whatever gifts we get.

Jesus surprised his friends with
fresh breakfast cooked over hot coals.

—John 21:9

Santa surprises naughty children
with fresh coal: whoa!

After a long day in court,
Jesus was once spotted
carrying a crossbar on his back.

—John 19:17

After a long day of carrying
around a sack on his back,
Santa was once spotted in a bar.

Jesus wept.

—John 11:35

Santa said, "You better not cry..."

Jesus stands at the door and knocks.

—Revelation 3:20

Santa just comes on in uninvited: "What's up?"

Chapter 4
SANTA

I've always wondered why we make Santa out to be the bad guy. What's the big deal? Saint Nicholas was, after all, a saint. So I decided to do a bit of research and dig up the story of Santa Claus, and you know what I found? Santa doesn't have just one story. Santa is a conglomeration of stories, a legendary being that has evolved over the years.

Along the way, pre-Christian practices, the story of Saint Nicholas (a fourth-century bishop), Norse mythology, Scandinavian folklore, Dutch immigrants in America, Washington Irving, Clement Moore, Thomas Nast, the Coca-Cola Bottling Company—and more—all made their contributions. Santa's popularity piggybacks on these contributions. So I want to take time now to briefly point out a few.

I. Nicholas: The Patron Saint

Nicholas served as bishop of Myra (Southwest Turkey) from a young age and worked his entire life, giving to the needy, protecting children and serving God. He was in and out of jail for his faith and still had time to work the occasional wonder.

Myra was a coastal city. For that reason, many of the myths about Nicholas closely link him to the sea. Stories abound of him saving sailors in storms. Most involve him using his mysterious powers to calm stormy seas, but there are also tales of him walking on water to reach drowning sailors and, on one occasion, even using prayer to bring back to life a sailor who died in a fall from a ship's mast. Naturally, it didn't take long for him to become known as the patron saint of sailors.

Nicholas is also popularly known as the patron saint of children. Many of his stories tell of children rescued from misfortune and returned to the safe care and keeping of their families. In France, the most familiar story, both told and sung, is of three little children lured into the clutches of an evil butcher and rescued by Nicholas.

In another story, Nicholas is said to have saved three poor sisters from slavery during the fourth century by dropping gifts of gold to them down through a chimney of the house in which they worked as domestic servants. The gold landed in a stocking that one of them had hung near the fireplace to dry. Thus, today, young girls and boys all over the world hang stockings, hoping that Santa will drop down gifts for them while they sleep on Christmas Eve.

Other stories tell of children who disappeared, were kidnapped, or fell into a well, all to be miraculously rescued and returned to safety because of the efforts and prayers of Saint Nicholas. Stories like these have emotional, universal appeal. No wonder he is known as the beloved patron saint of children.

As the years went on and his reputation spread, Nicholas ended up becoming the patron saint of a wide variety of groups, places, and causes. The list of things for which Nicholas has been declared patron saint is quite lengthy.

Interestingly, some of the things for which he has been declared patron saint contradict one another. For example, he is patron saint of both judges and murderers, both students and teachers, both wealthy oil traders and the poor. He's the patron saint of both brides and grooms, both unmarried men and unmarried women, both lovers and virgins, or, we might as well just say—everyone! Saint Nicholas is indeed just about everyone's saint. If there was a patron saint contest for "Who has the most credits to his name?" Saint Nicholas would win by a landslide.

II. Odin: The Norse Legend

Here comes trouble. This is where Christians usually draw the line when it comes to Santa's influence on Christmas—his ties to Odin. I made a crack earlier about Santa being Thor's father. If you have seen any of the Marvel Comics movies you may have picked up on that reference; in them you get an intimate look into the wild world of Asgard, where Odin is ruler and Thor is his most famous son.

Odin, the white-bearded god of gods in Norse and Germanic mythology, is the Hollywood star of the winter

Yuletide festivities. Somewhere along the way, Christmas, Saint Nicholas, and the legends of the Norse god crossed paths and got intertwined, and Odin, the lord of the Yule, was transformed into Father Christmas after Christianity reached the Germanic peoples. Believe it or not, there are a number of similarities between the Norse legend and the stories that surround Santa.

Odin was believed to visit at night, bringing gifts to the children; so does Santa. Odin delivered gifts while riding across the night sky on his *eight-legged* mythological horse with supersonic speed; Santa delivers gifts while riding across the night sky with the help of *eight reindeer* with supersonic speed. Odin had a long white beard; so does Santa. A sheaf of grain was left in the field for Odin's horse; our children sprinkle a vial of mixed grains and glitter outside in the yard for Santa's reindeer.

Some historians believe that, along with Odin's influence, attributes of the Germanic god Thor (the-god-of-thunder) were transferred to Nicholas too. Thor was supposedly older and heavy with a long white beard; he rode through the air in a chariot drawn by two white goats; he dressed in red; his palace was in the "northland;" he was friendly and cheerful; and he would come down the chimney into his element, the fire.

The similarities are striking, to say the least.

From Odin and Thor to modern-day Santa, the jolly old elf has come a long way. At the end of the day, I can understand why Odin's influence on the Santa tradition may make some parents re-think the role Santa plays in their Christmas celebrations.

III. Krampus: The Christmas Devil

Did you know that Santa has an evil helper? Well, evil helper may be the wrong word. Perhaps a better word would be *petrifying persuader*. So we know that Santa makes a list and checks it twice. On his list is an inventory of naughty and nice children. For the nice children, Santa brings gifts. But years ago, the naughty children faced a far worse fate than receiving a lump of coal. They had to face Krampus, the Christmas Devil, who *whips* and *scares* children into being nice.

The legend is part of a centuries-old Christmas tradition in Germany, where Christmas celebrations begin in early December. According to legend, Krampus shows up in towns the night before December 6, known as Krampus Night. December 6 also happens to be Saint Nicholas Day, when German children look outside their doors to see if the shoes they left out the night before contain either gifts (for good behavior) or sticks (for bad behavior).

Opposite the rosy-cheeked jolly ole' Saint Nick, Krampus is a beast-like monster, with hoofed feet, fangs, and goat horns, that comes with a bundle of sticks in hand, ready to swat naughty children, kidnap them, and take them to the underworld as his trophies. More ghastly than anything you would see on the streets during Halloween, Krampus is horrifying. So you can imagine how high the stakes were for the naughty kids. I mean, really. It just wasn't worth it to be naughty, not with Krampus on the loose!

The first question people usually ask after I explain Krampus is 'Did you make this up?' At which point I respond, no, I did not make this stuff up. His folklore tradition, which most likely originated from a well-known tale about Saint Nicholas' battle with the devil, has made its way to the United States where Krampus is gathering a cult-like following. He has made an appearance on the comedy channel and can even be found on Pinterest.

"If there's money to be made, people will find a way to make it," someone once said. Perhaps that explains why the *commercialization* of Krampus is also on the rise. In Europe, for example, in the same places where you can buy a Santa hat and wrapping paper, Krampus chocolates, Krampus figurines, and Krampus devil horns are for sale.

Think about that for a moment.

***

One of the things so fascinating about the evolution of Santa is the depth of discovery involved. For every one of his characteristics you identify and research, there seems to be another interesting trait, waiting for its chance to be seen and heard.

Jesus appealed to people's imagination
by telling parabolic stories.
Isn't Santa just another story that
appeals to our moral imagination?

Chapter 5
JESUS

When it comes to the story of Jesus, it would serve you well to look in the mirror and ask yourself, "Has Jesus shaped what I believe it means to live a Christian life?"

If your answer is yes, then the word I'm about to give you to help distinguish Jesus' story from Santa's story should make perfect sense—sacrifice. It's that word that defines the difference. The story of Jesus is a story about giving. And the story of Santa is a story about giving. The difference: Santa's gift only requires the sacrifice of time and effort, whereas Jesus' gift required the sacrifice of life—his life.

The story of Jesus is one about a man who was born in an obscure village, the child of a Hebrew woman. He grew up in another village, where he worked in a carpenter shop until he was thirty. Then, for three years, he was a traveling preacher with no place to call home. He never acquired wealth. He never held an office. He never traveled more than two hundred miles from the place where he was born. He did none of the things one usually associates with greatness.

He prayed for those who taunted him and showed compassion toward those who didn't even know him. He healed the people who came to him and prayed for future generations who would eventually know him. His follower's included wealthy business owners, fishermen, a tax collector, a zealot, a twin, and, only one he called friend, Judas.

Jesus was the kind of person who wasn't too worried about his reputation. He could talk academically with religious leaders one day, and sit down to dinner with notorious sinners and offer an unconditional ear the next. When it came to 'others,' Jesus was all-inclusive and didn't participate in the exclusion tactics that were popular in his day. He was a country boy who welcomed charity and dismissed rigidity in favor of mercy. He mingled with lame and blind, prostitutes and sinners, women and children (who, during that time, were treated as less than human) alike. He made a habit of treating everyone the same—with unconditional love and unparalleled respect.

He was only thirty-three when the tide of public opinion turned against him. He was handed over to his enemies and went through the mockery of a trial. He was nailed to a cross between two thieves. Upon his death, he was laid in a borrowed grave.

Centuries have come and gone, and yet, he remains the central figure of ethical teaching and the head of the Christian church.

Who has influenced *you* more, Jesus or Santa?

Chapter 6
Our Secular, Gift-Bearing Trinity

Every year, like clockwork, people all over the world unite to resurrect the spirit of Christmas. Homes are decorated with strings of lights. Black Friday deals turn our angst to smiles of delight. We are nicer to strangers. We start giving more than just nickels and dimes to charity. We ignore the fact that there's sap dripping from the fir tree and onto the floor. Holiday cheer fills the air—and it has power. No matter how much doom-and-gloom we see on the news. No matter how naughty or nice our children have actually been. Christmas always seems to provide just the right amount of kindness, generosity, and comfort.

Is Christmas the 'comforter' Jesus was talking about in John's gospel (John 14:16)? On the eve of his departure, Jesus told his followers that they would not be left alone, but that another Comforter (another Advocate) would come to assist them. This Comforter would be the Holy Spirit. The comfort Christmas provides, of course, was not what Jesus was talking about.

But, still, you have to admit, the annual Christmas spirit does seem to offer not just comfort, but also hope and forgiveness. Yes, Christmas even provides a dose of forgiveness. Every child sooner or later realizes that even if he or she has not been perfect all year, Santa still comes through. It's no wonder Christmas has become a religion.

RELIGION:

noun | re-lig-ion | \ri-ˈli-jən

4. A cause, a principle, or an activity pursued with zeal or conscientious devotion.

—*The American Heritage Dictionary*

Christmas has become a *hybridized* religion and has given birth to something new: a gift-bearing trinity. Instead of Father, Son, and Holy Ghost, we now have Santa, Toys and the Christmas Spirit. So how do we unravel this mix of tradition, legend, and religion that has become completely intertwined? You may not like my answer, but you have to start somewhere. The place to start is with—you.

The more we grow and the more we understand about ourselves, the more we can offer a foundation of emotional support that enables our children to grow.

Research in the field of child development has demonstrated that children's sense of security and connection to their parents is very closely related to the parents' understanding of and sense of security toward themselves.

The process of freeing yourself from patterns of the past begins by coming to terms with your past experiences (the bad ones as well as the good ones). Not taking time to look in the mirror and make an honest assessment will only bring about the fulfillment of the maxim "history repeats itself." If negative patterns from your past go unaddressed, they stand a good chance of being passed down to your children.

I think Naomi Aldort says it best in her book, *Raising Our Children, Raising Ourselves*. In the book she explains that we must first learn how to get our own emotional reactions and conditioning out of the way. Why? So that our children can be themselves without being held back by *our* pasts, *our* anxieties about the future, and *our* concerns about what others may say about us as parents.

You want to know how to unravel this Jesus versus Santa, sacred versus secular mixed-up mess? Get *you* out of the way. That's the first step to untying the knot. We must deal with our issues, fears, and egos first in order to move forward toward the healing we need. To say it in a slightly different way, "The one thing holding back my child from better understanding the most valuable traits of Jesus and Santa, is me."

In order to become all God wants us to be, we have to free ourselves from any unrealistic expectations we have placed on ourselves. With God's help, and through the work of the Holy Spirit, we can change the way we think, and in so doing, change how we live. While the secular trinity helps us strive to become better versions of ourselves temporarily (during the month of December), the real Trinity gives us the needed strength to change our courses in life, permanently.

Remember: Take time to reflect on how you experienced Christmas as a child. If that child was hurt or wounded, be a loving parent to that child now; take time to heal.

Recognize: The more deeply you dig, the more you may experience the peace which surpasses understanding, a way of living that begins from within.

Remember: The light you find is the light that has been waiting to be discovered. Claim it for yourself, but also share it with others.

Recognize: The Christmas season allows us time to enjoy an external spark and an internal awakening. Take advantage of this opportunity. Stop being an enemy to yourself.

Chapter 7
You Need to Read This!

"You need to clean your room," we tell our children.

"You need to eat your vegetables."

"You need to do your chores to get your allowance."

"You need to tell your sister that you're sorry."

"You need to be good to get a prize."

Have you ever considered how authoritative and controlling the word "need" is? Personally, I don't think we take the word seriously enough. A need is absolute, definitive, non-negotiable. I'm certain the word "need" doesn't need anyone telling it what it needs! Sadly, many in our world today focus so much on meeting their needs on the outside that they end up starving themselves to death of the needs they have on the inside.

"You just need to believe me when I tell you…"

If I had to guess, that is how many Christian parents begin their talk when the time comes. When that terrible-twos toddler one day becomes a little older and wiser and you sit him down and look him in the eyes and say: "You just need to believe me when I tell you there is no Santa. But Jesus, now he is real. He is God's son who died on a cross so that we might live with him in heaven after we die."

Straight to the point. No need for questions. "I just told

you everything you need to know." No room for your child to think and analyze on his own, no wiggle-room for debate (even though he likely has a ton of questions), just good ole' fashioned *That's the Facts, Jack, believe that.*

That is certainly one approach. But let's take another route.

Let's say you decide *not* to tell your child there is a difference between Jesus and Santa. Let's say we just let our children believe both are real. If you tell your children both are real, they will be faced with a serious dilemma once they figure out you were not completely honest with them. When the day comes that your children figure out you lied about Santa, what do you believe they will think about Jesus? How will an innocent tradition compromise their ability to trust you?

Hmmm, let's see, Mom and Dad lied to me about Santa, the Easter Bunny, and the Tooth Fairy, so there's a pretty good chance they're hiding something about this Jesus guy too. Rather than the traditional "'Twas the night before Christmas" refrain, your child might just mumble the following instead:

All through the night, I tried not to make a sound.
The only noise was my chest starting to pound.

I was excited my gift was finally on its way,
But Christmas morn' trickery came into play.

You cheated me, Santa, with this lump of coal.

In the chambers of my heart you left a big hole.

Christmas was fun, with presents galore,
But now I see what you've had in store.

The lies you fed me, the way that you grin,
I'll never forget this unforgivable sin!

Believe it or not, separating Santa from Jesus (and vice versa) may be more of a parenting challenge than you might think. Not because Jesus and Santa are topics too serious to tackle, but because the way you handle this subject will lay the groundwork for how you dismantle controversies and trust issues in your home for years to come.

Being a parent myself, I would not recommend just ripping the band-aid off but, rather, proceeding with caution and care. No parent wants to lie to their children. But on the other hand, no parent wants to burst the magical bubble that makes the holiday season so precious to them either. Before diving in, take time to consider the following:

Remember: Certainly we need to tell our children first and foremost that Christmas celebrates God's Son coming to earth. But other Christmas traditions also have the ability to enrich and bless a family's celebration. Don't throw the baby out with the bath water.

Recognize: Santa is not a holiday monster that smashes and destroys every meaningful thing there is about Christmas but, rather, an example of someone who brings you a gift you did not earn. Allowing children to experience generosity and grace at an early age can help them better understand Jesus' prodigal-son-type parables at a later stage.

Remember: It's okay to believe in the magic of Christmas: heartfelt hugs, waking to a surprise snowfall, unexpected acts of kindness, Christmas cards with well-thought-out, meaningful wording.

Recognize: It's okay to use Santa, not to make your kids behave, but to teach them to be more giving (which is an expression of love) rather than demanding it (which expresses selfishness). On this one thing Jesus and Santa would certainly agree, "It's more blessed to give than to receive" (Acts 20:35).

Chapter 8
Three Steps to a Healthy Coexistence

We live in a world where *quantity* and *quality* are easily confused. Value is measured in terms of amount, and people are constantly telling us that more is better. I have found the following three steps to be a wholesome, healthy approach. Here, now, are three quality ways to get you started down the road of reclaiming the Christ in Christmas while not shoving Santa off his sleigh, and doing it in a way your child will understand and value for years to come.

***

1) **READ.** Reading to your children is clearly a good idea. Every time we interact with our children, we have the opportunity to promote growth, either negative or positive. When reading to your child, quality is more important than quantity. Quality reading is not going over a bunch of information for your kids to assimilate, but an opportunity for you to make discoveries *with* your child, with you as the guide. Reading serves to create a healthy habit and gives us the chance to pass down something we value.

Begin by reading tales of Santa from a storybook and let

your child ask questions as you go. Tell your child a little bit of history about the story you selected. Where it originated, the legend it is based on. Even that what they are hearing (in some cases) is make-believe. They will not go into shock over hearing this. Trust me. Our kids come in contact with a whole slew of characters that are make-believe. From Big Bird to Mickey Mouse, to movies starring cats and dogs that talk, children understand and have the ability to differentiate far more than we give them credit for. If your kids happen to react anything like mine did, they probably won't even be surprised, not as much as you thought they would be anyway.

> Give your children freedom—when you
> hold them captive to your own expectations,
> you limit growth.

The next day when story time rolls around again, read the story of baby Jesus. It doesn't matter if you read the story from a children's Bible or an adult Bible, or if you would rather just listen to it being read on your favorite reading supported device. The main thing here is—balance. If you read about Santa in a popular Christmas story one day, make sure the next time around you read about Jesus.

If reading Jesus' birth story to them over and over again sounds boring—it is. But it doesn't have to be. There's more to it than that. Take time to do some research. Dig a little deeper. Tell your kids what you discovered. Elaborate. Tell them about the many different meanings and lessons found *behind the scenes* of Jesus' birth story.

To give you an idea of what I'm talking about, here are several questions you can do further research on to help get you started:

"What do the gifts the Magi bring (gold, frankincense, myrrh) teach us about Jesus?" "Who are the 'wise men' in your life that you look to for advice?" "Of all the people the angels could have visited, why did God send them to the shepherds?"

If you want to read the birth story that includes the visit of the *shepherds* turn to the gospel according to Luke 2:1–18. If interested in the story that includes the visit of the *Magi*, look in the gospel according to Matthew 1:18–25; 2:1–23.

As every parent and grandparent knows, children are not shy about asking questions. It doesn't matter to them if they don't fully understand something. If they have a question, they're going to ask it. So don't worry too much about whether or not your child is going to fully understand what you tell them.

**Trust your good intentions.
Don't *force* your good intentions.**

Perhaps nicest of all, reading encourages intimacy. It offers your child the chance to have your undivided attention and the comfort of your close proximity. What better way to strengthen your child's faith in God while exploring the traditions of Christmas? Don't be surprised when you begin to see improvements in your child's ability to understand why it's okay to write to Santa but only pray to Jesus.

***

2) **TALK.** Talk to your kids. It sounds almost silly having to say that, but look around. Social media is the primary tool we use to communicate. People don't talk to each other anymore. We text, tweet, "like," friend, and un-friend instead. We do more "selfie" sending and cloud-based gaming than we do face-to-face relating and in-the-same-room friendship creating.

I once saw a television special about a teenage couple who would sit in restaurants on their dates, in the same booth, at the same table, only inches away from each other, and *text* one another rather than talk to each other. Are we losing the ability to carry on conversations with one another? I hope not. Don't let that happen to you and your family. Talk to your children. I promise you, the return on your investment will be an abundance of priceless memories.

What should you talk about?

Talk—about holiday memories of the past. The holidays are prime time for talking. When you're in the car going over the hills and through the woods to grandma's house, while putting up the Christmas tree or having your holiday meal, share a story with your children. Leave in the funny bits, the sad bits, the gross and smelly bits; kids can tell when a story has been candy-coated for their protection. Then invite everyone else to tell a story. Don't forget the youngest and the oldest storytellers in the group. Their stories are oftentimes the truest and the most revealing.

Sharing holiday memories with your loved ones has the ability to inspire, protect, and bind people in ways that one-sentence text messages could never do. So be generous with talking about those stories you love. The only cost is your time. The payoff: your children will have them for a lifetime.

Another talking point—talk about talking to God. Don't just limit God-talk to Sunday. Most of us probably talk to God on a daily basis within our minds, or in the form of setting aside some time for prayer and devotion. So why not pass along this gift of communicating with the Divine to our children? And if we make a habit of regularly talking to our children throughout the course of the year about Jesus and God, it will make a huge difference in the long run, in the next year, when Christmas rolls around.

Talk—about the symbolic meaning behind many of the decorations we see at Christmas. Here is a brief synopsis of several to get you started:

The wreath, much like the wedding band that couples exchange when married, has no beginning and no end. So, too, the love which comes down at Christmastime is eternal.

Wreaths, therefore, symbolize the love of God, which never ends. Holly leaves are added to wreaths because of a story, which dates back to the first century, that says the crown of thorns worn by Jesus was mixed with holly. According to the same legend, the holly berries changed from red to white after his resurrection from the dead on Easter morning.

Lighted candles in windows at Christmas, aside from beautiful, are used by many Christians as symbols of Christ as the "Light of the World" (John 8:12). German storytellers describe how the Virgin Mary, accompanied by angels, crossed the countryside on Christmas Eve on her way to Bethlehem. They encourage children to place lighted candles in the windows of the homes to "light the way for the blessed Virgin" and to indicate to all other weary travelers that this is a home in which they can find shelter.

The Christmas tree is traditionally an evergreen, such as a spruce, pine, or fir. The evergreen tree has been a symbol for Christmas and the center of holiday festivities for many years. The green color of the tree symbolizes growth. The evergreen also represents everlasting life—always alive, even in the midst of winter.

Turn off the TV. Put down the iPhone. Be emotionally present. Seize the moment. Be yourself. Begin bridging the communication gap and prying open the door to a deeper bond with your kids by going back to the basics—talking.

Talk. Talk. Talk. And then talk some more.

***

3) **SHOW**. Show your children that there is a difference between the Santa we see in the mall on Saturday and the Jesus we sing about on Sunday. Whether we realize it or not, the *way* we live says something to our children. For example, to know love we must not only know about love, but we must act lovingly. Over and over again, the Bible teaches that the gospel is most intimately known by those who live it.

The spiritual foundation we want for our children later in life is built, in part, by how they see us living for Christ today. Children take note of what we say and do more closely than we think. Our responsibility as parents is to place our children on the path of Christ-like living.

Learn to view Christianity as a skill in holy living, rather than a task to be completed at all cost, or else. The show-by-doing principle, as you can imagine, does have its limits. We can become so preoccupied with doing things that we no longer have time to quietly receive God's word of grace and direction for our lives. Like the Pharisees, we can end up substituting our deeds for faith, or thinking that any kind of action will do. To say that doing good deeds is all there is to Christian living is not to tell the whole story. But it does tell part of the story.

By the things we do, we show our children
what the hands of God look like.

Show your children the impact Christ has had on your heart versus the impact Santa has had on your wallet. We can show the love of Christ in an infinite number of ways. In the way we talk *to* people and in the way we talk *about* people. In the way we choose to spend our time. In the way we give of our money. In the way we respect our friends. In the way we accept others. In the way we pray, and the list goes on.

> "Sometime, when you have a few moments, try to think of some other basic principle that would cure all the world's problems faster than the Golden Rule put into practice."
> —*Anonymous*

Far from being perfect parents, my wife and I continue to find creative ways of showing our children the true source of our inspiration for the things we do. Our hope is that they will see in us what God's hands and feet in action look like, and then strive someday to do the same.

Children are watching.

Be the person who offers a sincere smile and a welcoming hug. Be the person who offers a friendly handshake and a kind kiss goodbye. Build a home environment that makes everyone want to visit and no one want to leave. Be the person who visits the sick and calls those who live alone. That is what it means to live life following the way of Christ. We can say far more with our deeds than we could ever imagine. Your actions have power. The power to mold children, improve neighborhoods, even change the world. Look at the impact twelve disciples had on the world…and it hasn't been the same since.

Chapter 9
A "10-Step" Fail-Proof Process

Fix you first.

Be real.

Be reasonable.

Need less.

Love more.

Slow down.

Read regularly.

Talk generously.

Show profusely.

And last but not least:
Have fun!

Chapter 10
Works Consulted

Aldort, Naomi. *Raising Our Children, Raising Ourselves.* Book Publishers Network, 2009.

Day, Katie. *Difficult Conversations: Taking Risks, Acting with Integrity.* The Alban Institute, 2001.

James, William. *The Varieties of Religious Experience: A Study in Human Nature.* New York: The Modern Library, 1929.

Kolatch, Alfred J. *The Jewish Book of Why.* New York: Jonathan David Publishers, 1981.

Nissenbaum, Stephen. *The Battle for Christmas.* Vintage Books, 1997.

The New Catholic Encyclopedia. 15 volumes. New York: McGraw-Hill, 1967.

22458415R00049

Made in the USA
Middletown, DE
31 July 2015